Katy Perry

ABDO
Publishing Company

Big
Buddy BOOKS
Buddy Bios

by Sarah Tieck

VISIT US AT
www.abdopublishing.com

Published by ABDO Publishing Company, 8000 West 78th Street, Edina, Minnesota 55439.

Printed in the United States of America, North Mankato, Minnesota.
062011
032012

 PRINTED ON RECYCLED PAPER

Coordinating Series Editor: Rochelle Baltzer
Contributing Editors: Megan M. Gunderson, BreAnn Rumsch, Marcia Zappa
Graphic Design: Maria Hosley
Cover Photograph: *AP Photo*: Evan Agostini, File.
Interior Photographs/Illustrations: *AP Photo*: Evan Agostini (p. 17), Gregg DeGuire/PictureGroup via AP IMAGES (p. 9), Brian Dowling/PictureGroup via AP IMAGES (p. 26), Kristian Dowling/PictureGroup via AP IMAGES (p. 19), Peter Kramer/NBC NewsWire via AP Images (p. 20), Stacie McChesney/NBCU Photo Bank via AP Images (p. 13), Frank Micelotta/FOX/PictureGroup via AP Images (p. 17), Frank Micelotta/PictureGroup via AP IMAGES (p. 7), Chris Pizzello (p. 5), Matt Sayles (p. 29), Sipa via AP Images (p. 23), Mark J. Terrill (p. 15), The Canadian Press, Adrien Veczan (p. 24), Ian West/PA Wire URN:9079016 (Press Association via AP Images) (p. 25); *Getty Images*: Hulton Archive (p. 17), Jamie McCarthy/WireImage for Gigantic Perfume (p. 27), Rebecca Sapp/WireImage (p. 11).

Library of Congress Cataloging-in-Publication Data

Tieck, Sarah, 1976-
 Katy Perry : singing sensation / Sarah Tieck.
  p. cm. -- (Big buddy biographies)
 ISBN 978-1-61783-021-1
 1. Perry, Katy--Juvenile literature. 2. Singers--United States--Biography--Juvenile literature. I. Title.
 ML3930.P455T54 2012
 782.42164092--dc23
 [B]
                        2011018227

Contents

Singing Star

Katy Perry is a **pop** singer and songwriter. She has won awards for her hit albums and songs.

Katy is famous. She has appeared on magazine covers. And, she has been **interviewed** on popular television shows.

> Katy is known for her fun fashion style.

Family Ties

Katy Perry's real name is Katheryn Elizabeth Hudson. She was born in Santa Barbara, California, on October 25, 1984. Her parents are Keith and Mary Hudson. Katy's older sister is Angela. Her younger brother is David.

Katy's parents helped her get her start as a singer.

Growing Up

As a child, Katy loved music. She often listened to **gospel** music. She also took singing and dancing lessons. Katy's parents were **ministers**. Sometimes Katy sang during church.

Katy attended Dos Pueblos High School near Santa Barbara. She wanted to work in music. So, she left high school early and earned a GED.

In 2011, Katy brought her grandma Ann Hudson to the Grammy Awards.

Starting Out

Katy wanted to record music. Her parents knew people who worked in gospel music. So Katy traveled to Nashville, Tennessee, to work with them.

In 2001, Katy released a Christian music album. It did not sell very well. But, it helped Katy learn about recording and working in music.

Katy changed her appearance as she was becoming known. She dyed her hair darker and wore different makeup and outfits.

Big Break

Soon, Katy started singing **pop** music instead of **Christian** music. People noticed her talent. During this time, she began calling herself Katy Perry.

Katy got other chances to record albums. When they didn't work out, she was very disappointed. Still, Katy kept working on her music.

In 2008, Katy **released** her first **pop** album. It is called *One of the Boys*. Katy wrote or helped write every song on the album. Her songs became known for their fun, playful words.

Several songs on *One of the Boys* became hits around the world. In 2008, Katy was **nominated** for a **Grammy Award**.

In 2009, Katy performed at the Grammy Awards.

Pop Pinup

Katy is known for her style. She often wears fun, fancy costumes. People compare her look to some beautiful 1930s and 1940s actresses. These women often appeared on posters called pinups.

Actresses Priscilla Lane (*left*) and Betty Grable (*right*) were famous pinup models. Katy's clothing and hair are often similar to their style.

Katy's clothes are often fun and colorful.

New Opportunities

Before long, Katy gained many fans! In 2010, she **released** her second major album. It is called *Teenage Dream*.

For this album, Katy wrote or helped write songs about her life and ideas. She made sure they had a good dance beat!

When Katy performs songs from *Teenage Dream*, the stage and costumes often look like sweets!

In August 2010, Katy
performed live on *Today.*

Did you know...

Katy's song "California Gurls"
was on the television show *Glee*
after the 2011 Super Bowl. This
was an important show since
many people were watching.

Teenage Dream became a popular
album. It had several hit songs. These
included "California Gurls," "Teenage
Dream," and "Firework."

Soon, Katy was recognized for her
successful album. In 2010, she was
nominated for several awards, including
four **Grammy Awards**.

A Singer's Life

Katy works hard on her music. She writes songs for her albums. Then, she spends many hours recording them.

After **releasing** an album, Katy often goes on tour. Her shows include interesting, colorful costumes and dancing. Before **performing**, she learns dance moves and practices her songs.

22

In 2011, Katy headlined the California Dreams tour. She was excited to be the main singer for a whole series of concerts!

When she is on tour, Katy may spend months away from home. She lives on a tour bus and travels to cities around the world. She **performs** live concerts. Katy also attends events and meets fans. Her fans are often excited to see her!

Many fans want to take pictures with Katy.

While on a trip to India, Russell asked Katy to marry him. They were sitting on an elephant!

Off the Stage

In October 2010, Katy married **comedian** and actor Russell Brand. They traveled to India for their wedding.

When Katy is not working, she and Russell like to be at home. They have cats named Kitty Purry and Morrissey. They like to spend time with friends and family.

Katy has made a perfume! It is called Purr. The bottle looks like a cat.

27

Buzz

Katy's fame continues to grow. In 2011, she was the voice of Smurfette in the movie *The Smurfs*.

People are often surprised by Katy's fun music and style. Fans are excited to see what's next for Katy Perry. Many believe she has a bright **future**!

Snapshot

★**Name**: Katheryn Elizabeth "Katy Perry" Hudson

★**Birthday**: October 25, 1984

★**Birthplace**: Santa Barbara, California

★**Albums**: *One of the Boys, Teenage Dream*

Important Words

Christian (KRIHS-chuhn) relating to Christianity, a religion that follows the teachings of Jesus Christ.

comedian a person who uses funny talk and actions to make people laugh.

future (FYOO-chuhr) a time that has not yet occurred.

gospel a type of Christian music.

Grammy Award any of the awards given each year by the National Academy of Recording Arts and Sciences. Grammy Awards honor the year's best accomplishments in music.

interview to ask someone a series of questions.

minister a person who leads church worship.

nominate to name as a possible winner.

perform to do something in front of an audience. A performance is the act of doing something, such as singing or acting, in front of an audience.

pop relating to popular music.

release to make available to the public.

Web Sites

To learn more about Katy Perry, visit ABDO Publishing Company online. Web sites about Katy Perry are featured on our Book Links page. These links are routinely monitored and updated to provide the most current information available.

www.abdopublishing.com

Index